DEADLY DISEASES

POLIO

BY CAROL HAND

CONTENT CONSULTANT
Susan Hafenstein, PhD
Professor, Department of Medicine
Pennsylvania State University

Cover image: The poliovirus has a relatively simple structure, but it can have severe effects on human health.

Core Library
An Imprint of Abdo Publishing
abdobooks.com

abdobooks.com

Published by Abdo Publishing, a division of ABDO, PO Box 398166, Minneapolis, Minnesota 55439.

Printed in the United States of America, North Mankato, Minnesota.
102021
012022

THIS BOOK CONTAINS RECYCLED MATERIALS

Cover Photo: Kateryna Kon/Shutterstock Images
Interior Photos: AP Images, 4–5, 17, 20, 34–35, 38, 43; Bettmann/Getty Images, 8; Anja Niedringhaus/AP Images, 11; Album/Prisma/Science Source, 14–15; Red Line Editorial, 22; Ami Images/Science Source, 24–25, 45; Kateryna Kon/Science Photo Library/Alamy, 27; Hafenstein Lab at Penn State University, 29; Altaf Qadri/AP Images, 32

Editor: Arnold Ringstad
Series Designer: Ryan Gale

Library of Congress Control Number: 2021941221

Publisher's Cataloging-in-Publication Data

Names: Hand, Carol, author.
Title: Polio / by Carol Hand
Description: Minneapolis, Minnesota : Abdo Publishing, 2022 | Series: Deadly diseases | Includes online resources and index.
Identifiers: ISBN 9781532196614 (lib. bdg.) | ISBN 9781098218423 (ebook)
Subjects: LCSH: Poliomyelitis--Juvenile literature. | Poliomyelitis--History--Juvenile literature. | Infectious diseases--Juvenile literature. | Epidemics--History--Juvenile literature. | Communicable diseases--Epidemiology--Juvenile literature.
Classification: DDC 614.49--dc23

CONTENTS

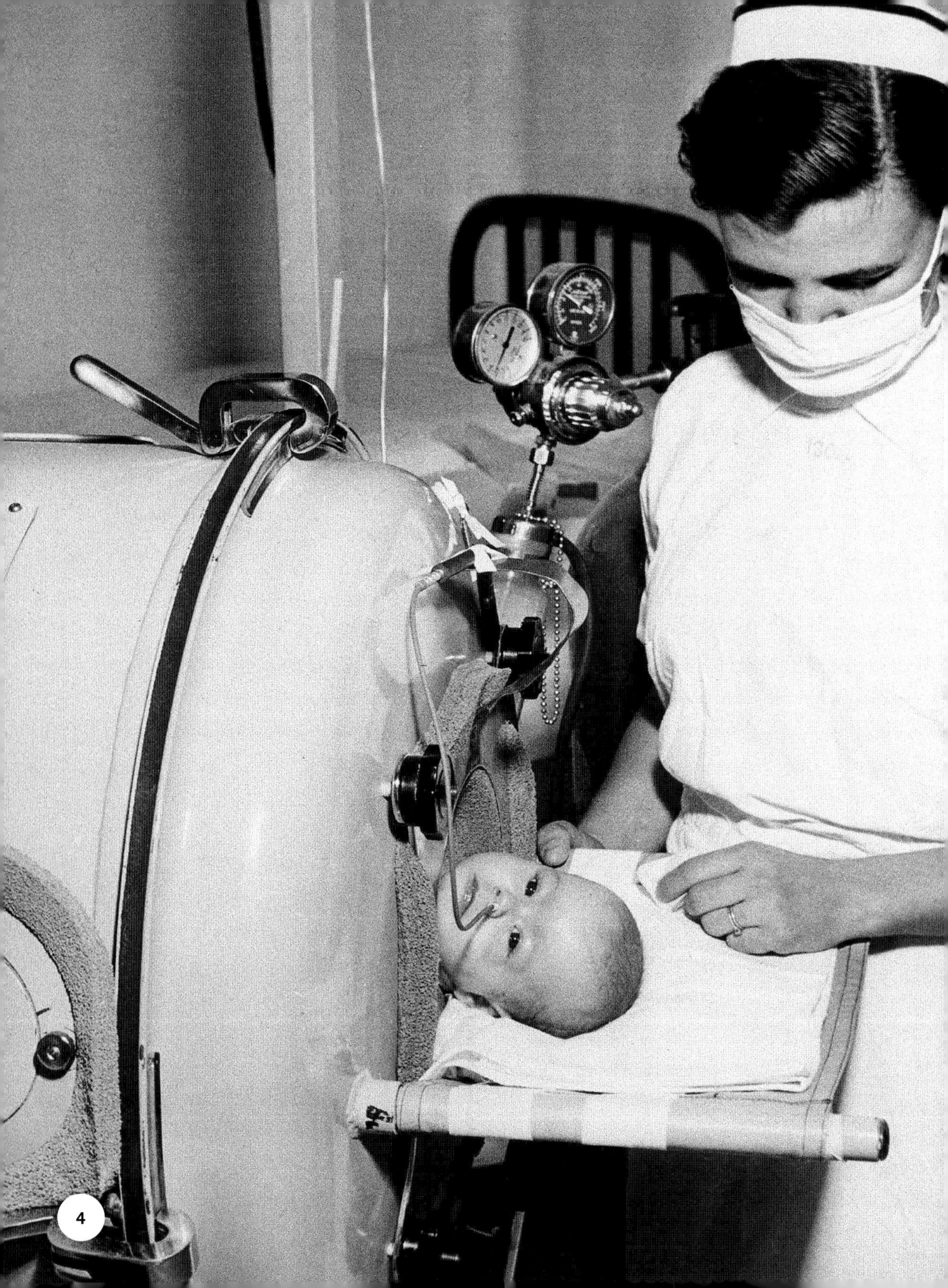

CHAPTER ONE

WHAT IS POLIO?

In October 1953, twins Frankie and Janice Flood were living in DeWitt, New York. They were first graders. They planned their Halloween costumes and hoped for lots of candy. But Frankie got a cold and had to stay home from school. On October 30, he was rushed to the hospital. Doctors diagnosed him with polio. He was quickly put in a machine called an iron lung. Only his head stuck out. The huge, yellow machine breathed for him. Polio had

In the 1950s, many babies and young children with polio were placed in iron lungs to keep them alive.

THE IRON LUNG

When breathing muscles are paralyzed, polio patients die of suffocation. To prevent this, Harvard professors Philip Drinker and Charles McKhann invented a breathing machine. It was first called the Drinker respirator. It later became known as the iron lung. It is a large, airtight tube that encloses the whole body except the head. It lowers pressure inside. This forces air into the lungs. Then pressure in the tube returns to normal. Air is pushed out of the lungs. Most polio patients spent one to two weeks in the iron lung. Their paralysis ended, and they could breathe on their own again. If paralysis continued, the patient might live in the iron lung for years. Iron lungs saved thousands of lives.

paralyzed his chest and throat muscles.

Doctors feared Janice had the disease too. On Halloween morning, they gave her several doses of gamma globulin. This is a mixture of antibodies found in human blood. Antibodies are proteins that protect the body from disease. The doctors hoped the gamma globulin would protect Janice from polio.

Sixty-one hours after Frankie entered

the hospital, he died. On the day he was buried, Janice went to the hospital. She had polio too.

Janice survived, but she lost her twin brother and best friend. Eight of Janice and Frankie's 24 classmates got polio that year. Most got better. But two of them later died. Janice spent many years learning to walk again.

THE POLIO SCARE

The Flood twins were two of more than 35,500 paralytic polio cases in the United States in 1953. Frankie was one of 1,450 deaths. The previous year, 1952, was the deadliest year for the disease. There were almost 58,000 US cases and 3,145 deaths. A series of severe polio epidemics began in 1916 and continued every summer across the country and world. Individual communities might suffer many deaths one year and few the next. The numbers in each area were unpredictable. But, overall, epidemics got worse every year.

The summer months were frightening. Summer was when most polio cases occurred. A child would appear to have the flu. Then the disease would turn deadly. To be safe, families did not go swimming or attend public gatherings. Parents insisted on frequent handwashing. In the early years of polio, most victims were under five years old. By the 1940s, most victims were aged five to nine. Boys were more likely to be paralyzed than girls.

PERSPECTIVES

MARCH OF DIMES

In 1938 President Franklin Delano Roosevelt founded the National Foundation for Infantile Paralysis (NFIP). He urged Americans to send dimes to the White House to fund polio research. Many radio and Hollywood personalities helped the effort. Radio personality Eddie Cantor coined the name March of Dimes. The campaign later became known by this name. Within a few weeks, the White House received 2,680,000 dimes, or $268,000. Over the years, the March of Dimes has raised millions of dollars.

President Franklin Delano Roosevelt visits with young polio patients.

A CONTAGIOUS DISEASE

Polio is short for poliomyelitis. It is a contagious disease caused by the poliovirus. This virus spreads from person to person. It affects the spinal cord. About 72 percent of people infected with polio have no symptoms. About 25 percent of people have flu-like symptoms that disappear after two to five days.

In rare cases, people infected with polio develop serious symptoms. These affect the brain or spinal cord. Infected people may suffer paresthesia, a feeling of having pins and needles in the legs. About four percent of infected people get meningitis. This is an infection of the covering of the brain or spinal cord. Paralysis is the most severe symptom. It occurs in one-half of one percent of infected people, or about one in 200. It can lead to permanent disability or death. If breathing muscles are paralyzed, the person often

In the United States polio is largely a thing of the past, but the disease still exists in a few countries, including Afghanistan.

dies. This happens to about two percent of people who become paralyzed.

Polio mostly affects young children. It is sometimes called "infantile paralysis." Muscles of paralyzed arms and legs become weak. They waste away over time because they cannot be used. Janice Flood is one of many polio survivors. She is now Janice Flood Nichols, a wife, mother, and social worker. She has spoken out about continuing efforts to fight polio. She believes that science can end the disease for good.

STRAIGHT TO THE SOURCE

Janice Flood Nichols contracted polio in 1953 and survived. Below, she explains what life was like when polio was causing yearly epidemics:

> *Parents lived in fear of warm weather—polio weather. They adhered to all public health recommendations and warnings: Avoid large public gatherings, never allow children to swim in public swimming pools, and insist upon frequent hand washing. One of my peers remembers that her mother forbade her to eat peaches in the summer for fear that the virus could flourish in the "peach fuzz." Another friend was forbidden to attend church each Sunday during the summer months. As children born soon after the end of [World War II], we were too young to appreciate our parents' terror. For us, "polio weather" was a terrible annoyance. Every time we turned around, our parents were curtailing our activities.*

Source: "Perspective of a Polio Survivor." *Children's Hospital of Philadelphia*, 11 May 2020, chop.edu. Accessed 25 June 2021.

BACK IT UP

What is the main point of the paragraph above? How does the author support this idea? Give two or three supporting details.

CHAPTER TWO

THE HISTORY OF POLIO

Humans may have suffered from polio for thousands of years. An Egyptian carving from about 1450 BCE shows a young man with a withered leg. This condition is typical of polio. The carving may represent the disease. But polio remained rare until the end of the 1800s. The first significant polio outbreak in the United States occurred in 1894. It happened in Rutland County, Vermont. Eighteen people died, mostly young children, and 132 were paralyzed.

An ancient Egyptian carving may show a young man with polio.

LEARNING ABOUT POLIO

Dr. Michael Underwood, a British physician, first described polio in 1789. He wrote that the disease affects the legs. Studies in 1905 by a Swedish doctor, Dr. Ivar Wickman, proved that polio was contagious. Dr. Wickman defined different types of polio, including paralytic and nonparalytic. He also stressed that infected people with no symptoms could spread the disease without knowing.

In 1908 Austrian physicians Karl Landsteiner and Erwin Popper identified the virus that causes polio. In 1931 Australian scientists Frank M. Burnet and Jean Macnamara found evidence of three types of poliovirus. These were named types 1, 2, and 3. The scientists showed that monkeys could recover from one type of poliovirus and still be infected by another type. Twenty years later, David Bodian and Isabel Morgan found more evidence for the three types of virus. In 1948 Thomas Weller and Frederick Robbins grew the poliovirus in

Karl Landsteiner helped discover the poliovirus.

living cells. Their studies laid the groundwork for later vaccine research.

POLIO EPIDEMICS

Polio was one of the most feared diseases in the world in the early 1900s. Polio epidemics paralyzed hundreds of thousands of children every year. In the summer of 1916, there was a major outbreak in Brooklyn,

MORE SERIOUS THAN POLIO?

People were terrified of polio. It showed up suddenly and no one knew why. Although it did not harm most people, it could cause paralysis or death. But many doctors disliked the emphasis placed on polio. They thought research should concentrate on more dangerous diseases, such as tuberculosis. In 1950 tuberculosis killed 34,000 people in the United States. In 1957 a deadly flu epidemic killed 62,000 Americans. But the number of annual polio deaths rarely exceeded a few thousand.

New York. More than 2,000 people died in New York. Across the country, more than 6,000 died. Thousands more were paralyzed. This was the first of the annual epidemics that repeated for decades. In the summer of 1921, Franklin Delano Roosevelt, who later became president of the United States, fell ill. His doctor diagnosed him with polio. He was paralyzed and used a wheelchair to move. The epidemics grew in size in the late 1940s and early 1950s. Tens of thousands of people were infected each year.

People knew a virus caused polio. But they did not know how it spread. They wrongly blamed immigrants, cats, car exhaust, and insects such as mosquitoes. Mosquito populations and polio cases rose in the summer. To guard against this possible cause, communities were sprayed with the toxic pesticide DDT. Parents tried to protect their children by keeping them clean and well rested.

Other parents tried to keep their children safe using what is now called social distancing.

PERSPECTIVES

ANNE WAFULA STRIKE

Born in Kenya, Anne Wafula Strike contracted polio at age two. Her family was forced from their home by superstitious neighbors. Even though she got better, life was a struggle. Anne always felt like an outsider. Today she lives in Harlow, in the United Kingdom. She is paralyzed and uses a wheelchair. She became a British Paralympian, competing in wheelchair racing. She works with the British Polio Fellowship to raise awareness of polio. Anne says, "While I may be disabled by polio, I am enabled by my determination."

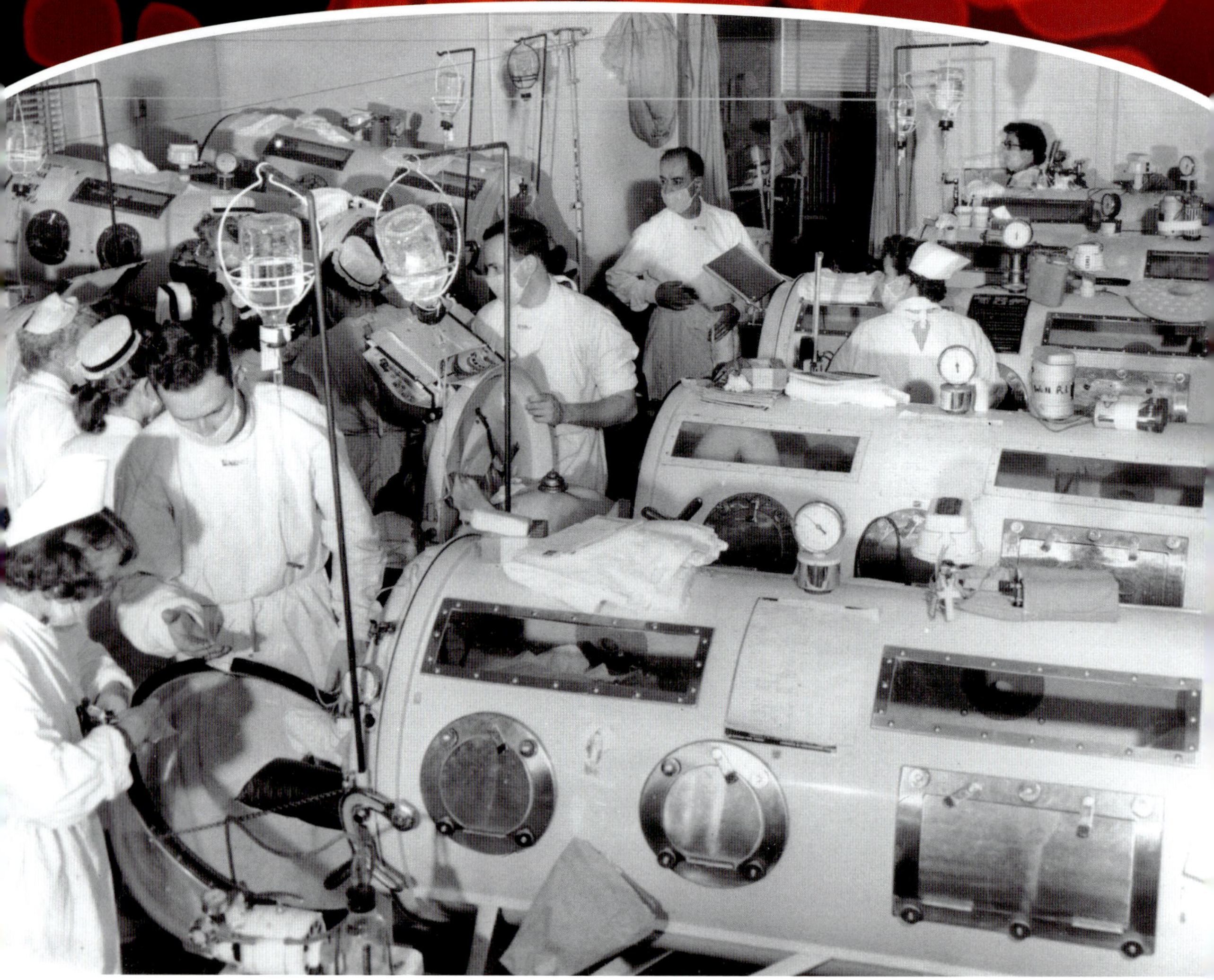

Hospitals filled with polio patients in the 1940s and 1950s.

Cities closed swimming pools, movie theaters, schools, and churches to prevent children from interacting. But people wanted a permanent solution to polio. They needed vaccines.

VACCINES TO THE RESCUE

Scientists had been researching polio vaccines for years. Jonas Salk worked at the University of Pittsburgh. He developed a vaccine from a killed poliovirus. On April 12, 1955, the government approved Salk's vaccine. Around the world, people proclaimed victory over polio. Salk refused to patent his vaccine, saying it belonged to the people. People received more than 400 million doses between 1955 and 1962. This reduced the number of polio cases by 90 percent.

Albert Sabin also developed a polio vaccine. His vaccine used a weakened form of the virus. Many people thought this would provide a longer immunity from polio than a killed virus. His vaccine was approved in the United States in 1961. It later replaced the Salk vaccine.

People around the world have been vaccinated for polio. US children must receive a complete series of polio vaccines before entering elementary school.

US POLIO CASES 1945–1965

The graph shows the number of polio cases in the United States from 1945 through 1965. The Salk polio vaccine was introduced in 1955. The Sabin vaccine was introduced in 1961. How does the graph demonstrate the effect of the vaccines on polio in the United States?

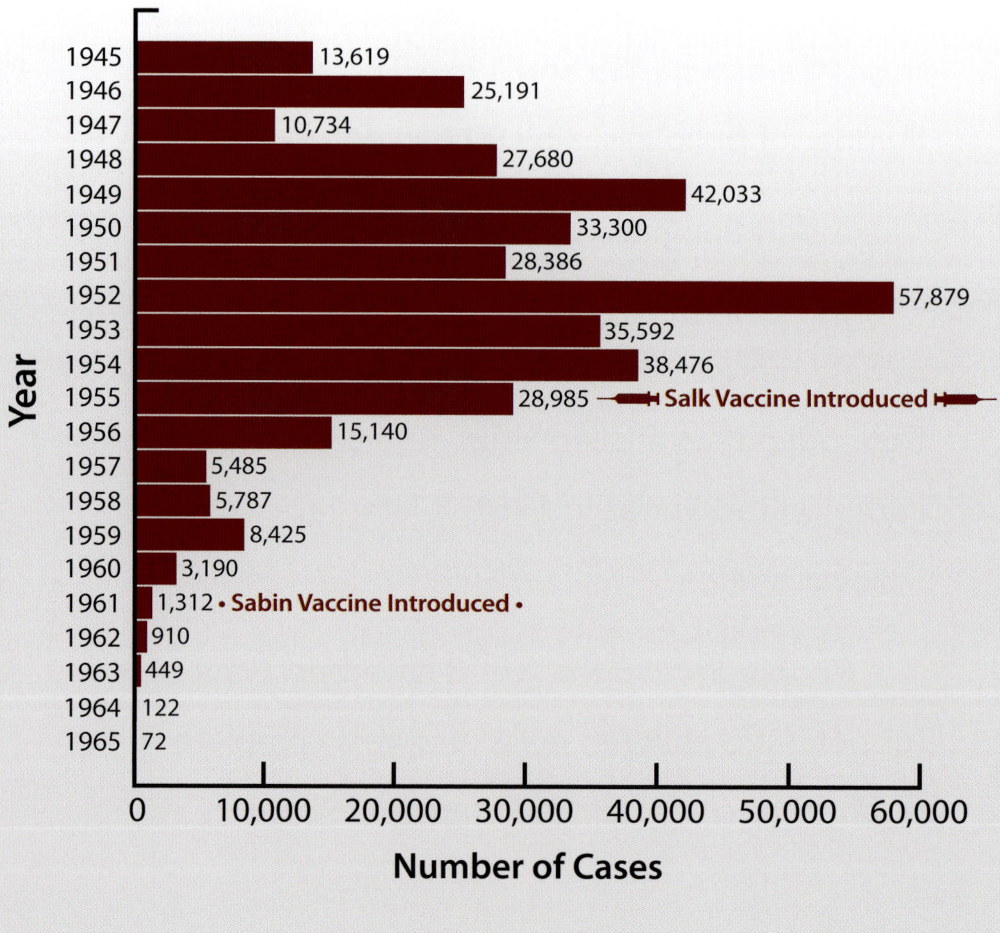

The Western Hemisphere was declared polio-free in 1994. By 2016, polio was spreading only in Afghanistan, Pakistan, and Nigeria. On World Polio Day, October 24, 2019, the World Health Organization (WHO) spoke about the disease's status. It said that there were only 94 cases of wild polio remaining in the world. Polio seemed to be nearing eradication.

FURTHER EVIDENCE

Chapter Two examines the history of polio. Identify the main point of this chapter and list several pieces of evidence supporting it. Then, visit the website below. Does the information on the website support the main point of the chapter? Does it present new evidence?

HISTORY OF POLIO

abdocorelibrary.com/polio

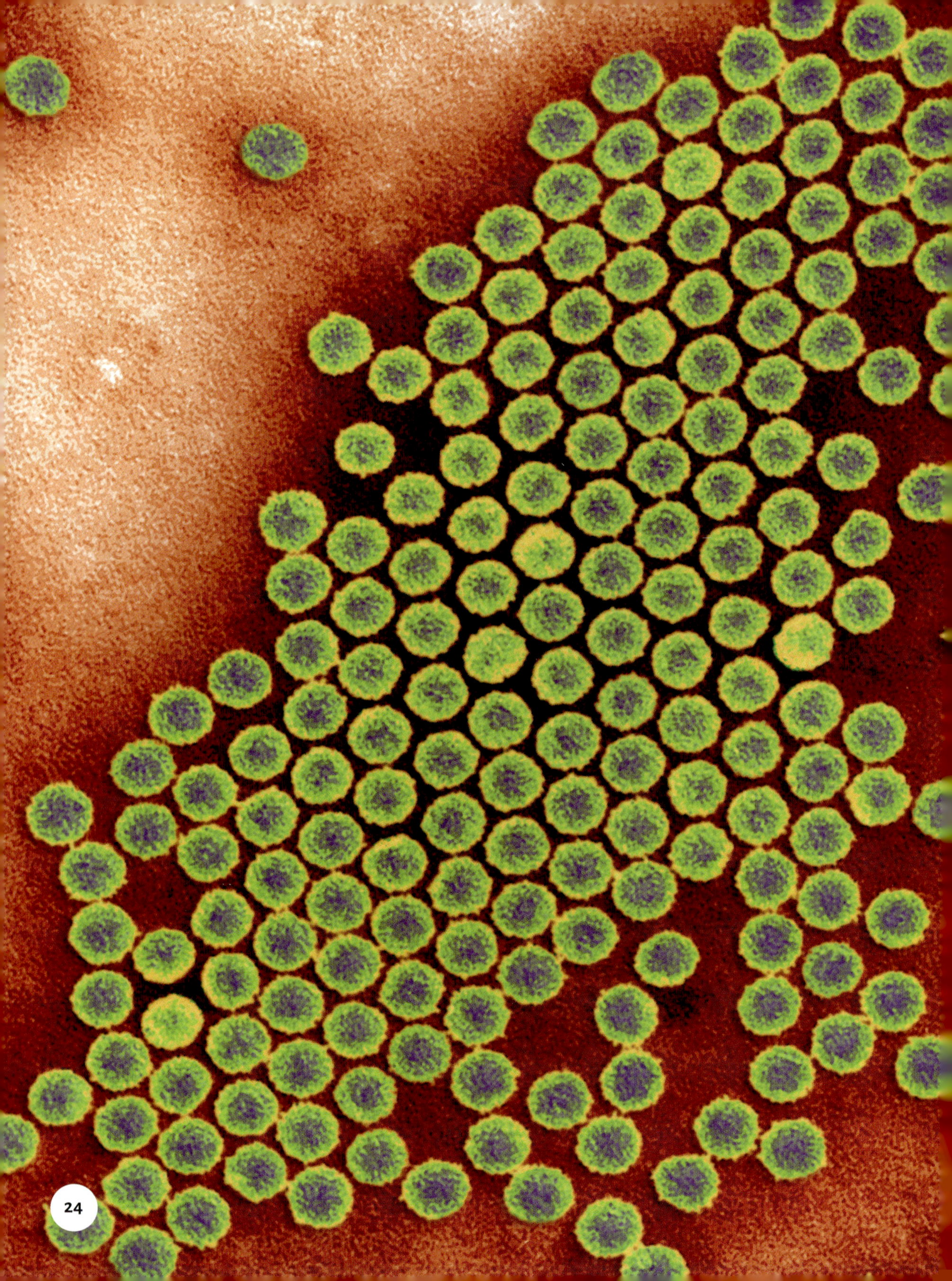

CHAPTER THREE

THE SCIENCE OF POLIO

Because polio is caused by a virus, there is no cure. The body's immune system must fight the disease on its own. The best way to fight polio is to prevent it. This can be done by either avoiding infection or being vaccinated. Polio passes easily from person to person. In most cases it causes few or no symptoms. But serious cases can lead to paralysis or even death.

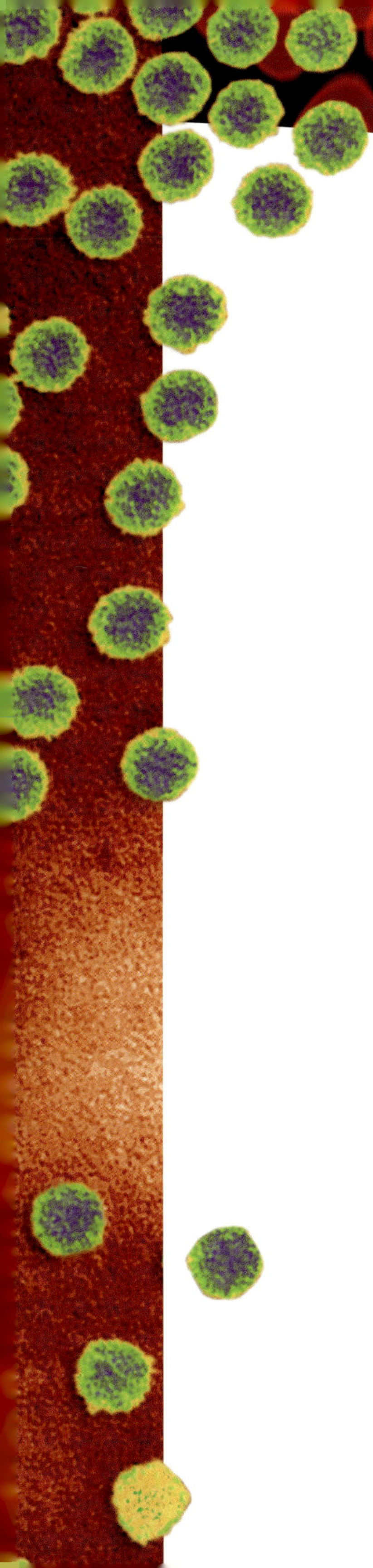

Powerful microscopes are needed to see the individual viruses that cause polio.

POLIO VS. COVID-19

Polio is mostly gone from the world, but a different epidemic began in 2019. COVID-19 mostly affects the elderly rather than young children. It spread rapidly across the world, while polio outbreaks were localized. Both are viral diseases. They cannot be cured, only prevented by vaccinations. Before vaccines were available for COVID-19, people practiced social distancing and washed their hands. They also wore face masks. Today, quick disease testing and rapid news reporting keep people better informed about outbreaks. Advances in science meant that making COVID-19 vaccines took months rather than years.

TRANSMITTING POLIO

The poliovirus is present in the feces of infected people. Some places do not have clean sanitation or safe ways to treat sewage. The virus can spread into the water supply or into food. It can also spread by close contact with an infected person. Infected people can spread the virus for weeks, even without showing symptoms. The virus enters through the mouth and

Unclean sources of drinking water can spread the poliovirus.

nose, infecting the digestive and respiratory systems. It multiplies in the throat and intestines. It can spread into the bloodstream. When it attacks the nervous system, it multiplies and destroys motor neurons. These are the nerves that control actions such as walking, swallowing, and breathing.

The virus can survive only in humans, not in other animals. Polio has a long incubation period, lasting up to ten days. This is the time between when a person is infected and when they show symptoms. Sometimes people have no symptoms at all, so the disease can spread for months without notice. The WHO says that finding even one case of polio in a country thought to be polio-free could signal an outbreak. If this happens, the WHO recommends declaring a public health emergency.

POLIOVIRUS

The poliovirus is a type of virus called an enterovirus. It is spherical in shape. The virus contains RNA as its genetic material. The RNA is enclosed in a capsid, or protein shell. Wild poliovirus exists in three forms: type 1, type 2, and type 3. Each type has only slight differences in its capsid protein. Still, the body sees them as different viruses. Being immune to one type does not make a person immune to the others.

Nerve cells have various proteins on their surfaces that stick out. One of these proteins works as a

STRUCTURE OF THE POLIOVIRUS

The diagram shows the major features of the poliovirus, a member of the *Enterovirus* genus. The poliovirus consists of a segment of RNA surrounded by a capsid. How does this diagram help you better understand how the poliovirus works?

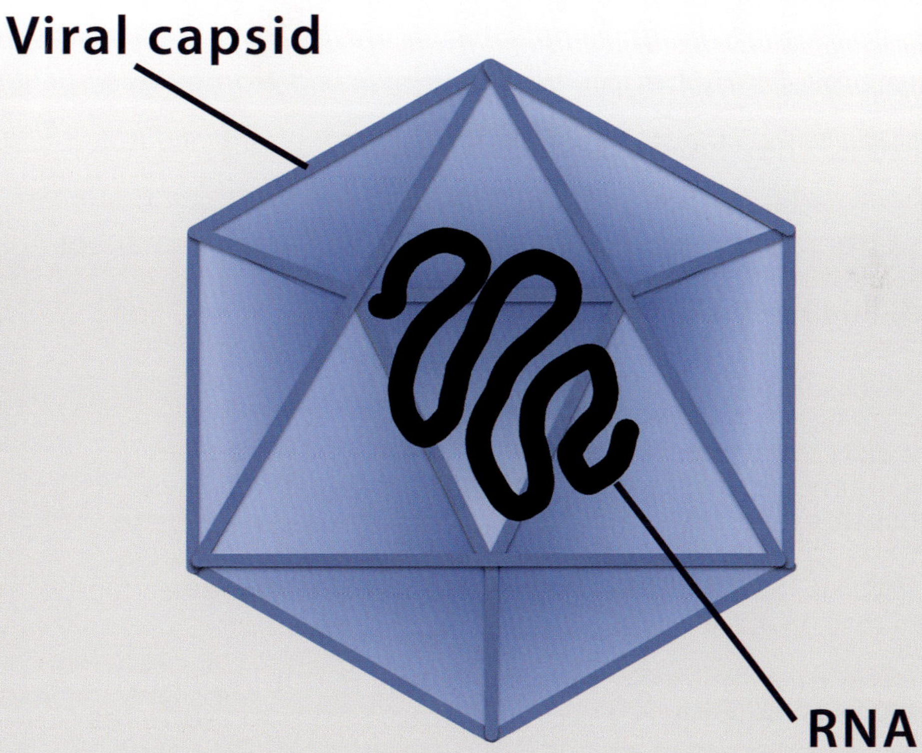

receptor protein. The poliovirus attaches to a nerve cell's receptor proteins. Then it enters the cell. It uses the cell's materials to make new viruses. In six to eight hours, each virus can make 10,000 to 100,000 new viruses. This kills the cell. The new viruses spread to other cells, infecting and killing them as well.

POLIO CATEGORIES

Polio is classified into categories based on its symptoms. Many people who are infected do not even realize it. They have no symptoms.

Others contract nonparalytic polio. This form causes mild, flu-like symptoms. These may include fever, sore throat, vomiting, headache, and fatigue. The person may also feel muscle weakness. There may be pain and stiffness in the neck, arms, legs, and back. These symptoms last up to ten days and then disappear.

The most severe polio infections result in paralytic polio. This occurs in about 0.5 percent of polio cases. These infections also begin with flu-like symptoms.

But within a week, the person begins to suffer severe muscle pain, spasms, and weakness. The person loses reflexes and experiences loose and floppy limbs. Sudden paralysis may occur. Body parts such as the hips, ankles, and feet may become deformed.

Paralysis affecting the spinal cord is called spinal polio. It causes paralysis in the arms and legs, along with breathing problems. Paralysis in the brain stem is bulbar polio. It affects sight, taste, swallowing, and breathing. If both the spinal cord and

PERSPECTIVES

POST-POLIO SYNDROME

Sometimes polio survivors develop symptoms called post-polio syndrome, or PPS. This can happen 15 to 40 years after recovering from the disease. The person may have symptoms such as muscle weakness, muscle wasting, breathing or swallowing problems, pain, and fatigue. Micki Minner is a PPS sufferer. She helps run an organization that supports polio survivors, including those with PPS. She says, "Our goal is to help polio survivors live a better life."

Paralytic polio can cause severe challenges in the daily lives of survivors.

the brain stem are involved, it is called bulbospinal polio, and the person has symptoms of both.

Before the 1900s, poor sanitation meant that most people were exposed to wild poliovirus as babies. They developed immunity or had immunity from their mothers, and polio epidemics did not occur.

As sanitation improved, children were older when first exposed. Their immunity against the virus was not as strong. More paralysis began to occur. Thanks to intensive vaccination programs, poliovirus type 2 was declared eliminated from the world in September 2015. The last case had been discovered in India in 1999. Type 3 wild virus was last detected in November 2012. It was declared eradicated in October 2019. In 2021, only type 1 wild virus still existed.

EXPLORE ONLINE

Chapter Three discusses the science behind how the poliovirus works. Visit the website below, which goes into more detail on this topic. Does the website answer any questions you had about the poliovirus? What new information did you learn from the website?

HOW THE POLIOVIRUS WORKS

abdocorelibrary.com/polio

CHAPTER FOUR

TREATING POLIO

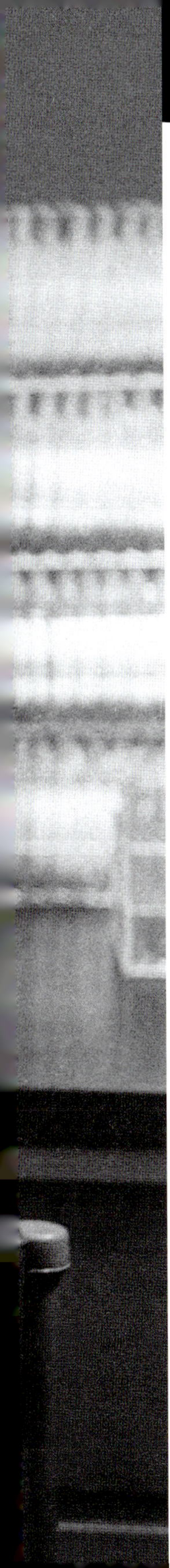

Scientists think polio first appeared after people began to live in cities. This allowed the virus to pass from person to person. Before vaccines were developed, the best way to slow polio's spread was to separate people. That way they could not pass it on. Vaccines were developed in the 1950s. Polio has now been eliminated from most of the world.

The polio vaccines developed by Jonas Salk, *pictured*, and Albert Sabin helped humanity fight back against polio.

POLIO AND TRAVELERS

The United States has been polio-free since 1979, but the risk of getting polio is not zero. A traveler can bring polio into the country. This happened in 1993. People who have not had the polio vaccine are at the highest risk of getting polio this way. People traveling out of the United States into countries where polio still occurs are also at risk.

PREVENTION AND TREATMENT

Before polio vaccines were available, people tried to prevent polio through lifestyle choices. They washed their hands frequently. They touched their eyes, noses, and mouths only with clean hands. People covered their mouths while coughing or sneezing. They avoided close contact with anyone who was sick. They did not consume food or drinks that might have been contaminated by someone with polio.

But people sometimes got polio even when they took these steps. Doctors focused on making patients comfortable and treating the symptoms. They tried to speed patients' recovery and prevent further issues. They used pain relievers and ventilators to help with breathing. Physical therapy helped with mild breathing problems. It also limited damage to the arms and legs. Other treatments included bed rest, heating pads, and drugs to relax muscles. Leg braces or wheelchairs helped patients get around.

When vaccines were developed, they became the best method of prevention. People must check with a doctor regularly to be sure their vaccinations are up to date. They must also get booster shots when necessary.

VACCINES

Two different types of vaccines have been developed. Jonas Salk's polio vaccine is known as the inactivated polio vaccine (IPV). It uses killed polioviruses. However, producing it requires a very large amount of virus. This is because the killed virus cannot reproduce in the body. This also makes the vaccine safe. If the virus cannot reproduce, it cannot cause the disease. The Salk vaccine

Once polio vaccines became available, many people waited in long lines to get the popular shots.

protects against all three types of poliovirus. It requires several doses to create immunity. Patients are given the vaccine by injection.

Albert Sabin's polio vaccine is the oral polio vaccine (OPV). It uses weakened versions of live polioviruses. This leads to lifelong immunity after one or two doses. The weakened virus can reproduce in the body very slowly. In extremely rare cases it may cause polio rather than preventing it. Between 1961 and 1989 in the United States, an average of nine people a year got polio after receiving the OPV. This vaccine is administered orally, by giving drops or putting it on a sugar cube.

The IPV was designed to protect only the nervous system. Because the OPV was taken by mouth, it also protected the digestive tract. It was easier and cheaper to vaccinate people with the OPV. It was also more effective at preventing the spread of polio. The OPV is the vaccine responsible for greatly reducing polio infections around the world.

> **PERSPECTIVES**
>
> **REPLACING THE OPV**
>
> David Salamone contracted polio as an infant after being given the OPV. Later he was diagnosed with an immune condition that made him likely to contract infections, including polio. Because of his experience, the Salamone family campaigned to replace the OPV with the IPV. The CDC made this change in 2000. Since then, no American child has contracted polio from a vaccine. The Salamone family's work has helped to change vaccination policy in many countries. David died in 2018 at age 28 of complications from his immune disorder.

WIPING OUT POLIO

Public health workers tirelessly fight to wipe out deadly diseases across the world. This requires vaccinating most of the world's people. Due to extensive vaccination, the last naturally occurring case of polio in the United States happened in 1979. In 1988 the United Nations and other organizations launched the Global Polio Eradication Initiative (GPEI). At that time, the disease was present in 125 countries. Since the GPEI began, wild polio cases around the world have decreased by 99.99 percent.

There is a very small chance people may get polio from the OPV. In 2012, the GPEI set a goal of phasing out the OPV and returning to the IPV. This would eliminate both the wild poliovirus and the vaccine-caused disease. The GPEI's ultimate goal is to eliminate polio from the planet. By 2021, that goal had nearly been achieved.

STRAIGHT TO THE SOURCE

Larry Rossini is a survivor of the 1950s polio epidemic. Writing during the COVID-19 pandemic of 2020, he compared the usefulness of vaccines in past and present pandemics:

> *I was a school child when the last widespread killer virus rampaged across the United States. . . .*
>
> *By now, most countries, including the U.S., have successfully eradicated polio through broad use of the vaccine, which was introduced in trials in 1955. Scientific studies have shown repeatedly that vaccines are the best way to squelch any communicable disease, including polio, and until the vaccination and pharmaceutical advances of recent decades, what we're now calling "social distancing" was the only way to ensure you wouldn't get infected.*

Source: Larry Rossini. "Message from a Past Epidemic." *The Public Interest Network*, 13 May 2020, medium.com. Accessed 2 Aug. 2021.

WHAT'S THE BIG IDEA?

Read the primary source text above. Determine the main idea of this selection, and list details supporting the main idea.

IMPORTANT DATES

1908
Austrian physicians Karl Landsteiner and Erwin Popper identify the poliovirus.

1916
A major polio outbreak occurs in Brooklyn, New York.

1938
President Franklin D. Roosevelt founds the National Foundation for Infantile Paralysis (NFIP), later called the March of Dimes.

1948
Thomas Weller and Frederick Robbins first grow the poliovirus in living cell cultures.

1955
On April 12, Jonas Salk's inactivated polio vaccine (IPV) is approved. A massive vaccination campaign begins.

1961
Albert Sabin's oral polio vaccine (OPV) is approved for use. It is cheap and quick to administer, and it quickly becomes the preferred vaccine around the world.

1988
The Global Polio Eradication Initiative (GPEI) is started by the United Nations and other organizations. The goal is to eliminate polio worldwide.

2015
In September, poliovirus type 2 is declared eliminated from the planet.

2019
In October, poliovirus type 3 is declared eliminated from the planet.

STOP AND THINK

Surprise Me

After reading Chapter Two on the history of polio, list two or three things that surprised you. Write a few sentences about each fact. Why did you find each fact surprising?

Dig Deeper

After reading this book, what questions do you still have about what it was like to have polio? With the help of an adult, find several reliable sources that can help answer your questions. Write a paragraph about what you learned.

Another View

Chapter One discusses the use of the iron lung to help polio patients. As you know, every source is different. Ask a librarian or another adult to help you find another source about this topic. Write a short essay comparing and contrasting the new source's point of view with that of this book's author. What is the point of view of each author? How are they similar and why? How are they different and why?

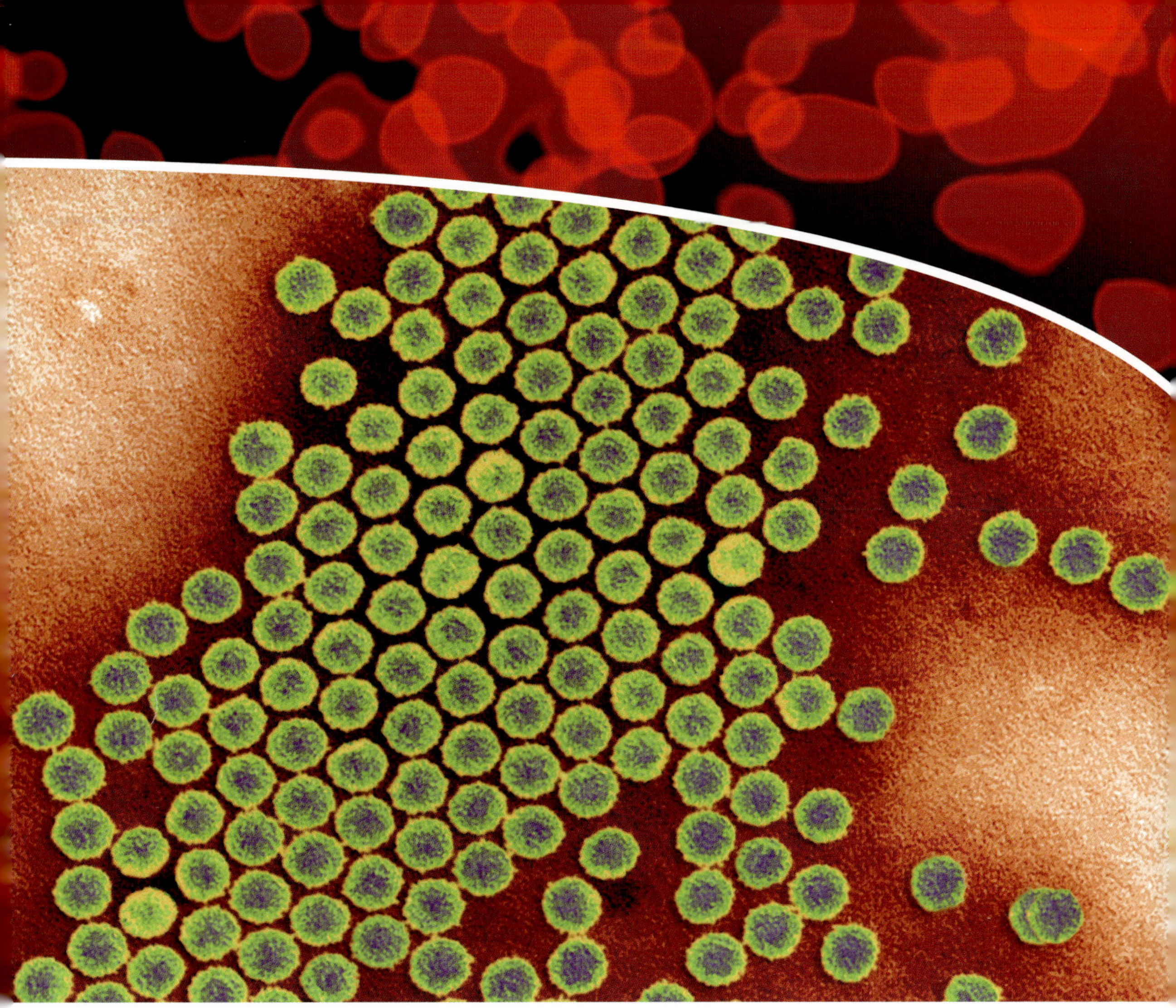

You Are There

Imagine you are transported back to the summer of 1952. Parents are terrified that their children will contract polio. Write a letter to your best friend in the future, describing what you experience. What is life like as a kid during a polio epidemic? How would your daily life differ from your life in modern times?

GLOSSARY

antibodies
proteins in the blood that help the body fight disease

contagious
easily passed from person to person

epidemic
a sudden increase in the number of cases of a disease

meningitis
an inflammation of the covering of the brain or spinal cord because of an infection

outbreak
a sudden increase in the occurrence of a disease

paralysis
inability to move the arms, legs, or other muscles, caused when the spinal cord is damaged by disease or injury

poliovirus
a type of enterovirus that causes poliomyelitis, or polio

social distancing
limiting the spread of a disease by avoiding close contact with other people

vaccine
a medicine that helps a person's immune system prepare to fight a disease

ONLINE RESOURCES

To learn more about polio, visit our free resource websites below.

Core Library CONNECTION
FREE! COMMON CORE MULTIMEDIA RESOURCES

Visit **abdocorelibrary.com** or scan this QR code for free Common Core resources for teachers and students, including vetted activities, multimedia, and booklinks, for deeper subject comprehension.

Booklinks NONFICTION NETWORK
FREE! ONLINE NONFICTION RESOURCES

Visit **abdobooklinks.com** or scan this QR code for free additional online weblinks for further learning. These links are routinely monitored and updated to provide the most current information available.

LEARN MORE

Gunderson, Megan M. *Franklin D. Roosevelt*. Abdo, 2021.

Nardo, Don. *How Vaccines Changed the World*. ReferencePoint Press, 2019.

INDEX

About the Author

Carol Hand has a PhD in zoology. She has taught college biology, written biology assessments, written middle and high school science curricula, and authored young adult science books, including several on health-related topics. Currently she works as a freelance science writer.